I Am NOT a Chicken

ANIMALS ON THE FARM

BY MARI BOLTE

Published by Pebble, an imprint of Capstone
1710 Roe Crest Drive, North Mankato, Minnesota 56003
capstonepub.com

Copyright © 2024 by Capstone. All rights reserved. No part of this publication may be reproduced in whole or in part, or stored in a retrieval system, or transmitted in any form or by any means, electronic, mechanical, photocopying, recording, or otherwise, without written permission of the publisher.

Library of Congress Cataloging-in-Publication Data is available
on the Library of Congress website
ISBN: 9780756573775 (hardcover)
ISBN: 9780756573720 (paperback)
ISBN: 9780756573737 (ebook PDF)

Summary: Lots of animals live on the farm. Follow the clues throughout the text and see if you can guess which animal is described.

Editorial Credits
Editor: Christianne Jones; Designer: Bobbie Nuytten; Media Researcher: Rebekah Hubstenberger; Production Specialist: Whitney Schaefer

Image Credits
Getty Images: Andras Jancsik, 16, 27 (top right), cinoby, 30, Pam Wright/EyeEm, 24, 27 (bottom right), Photos by R A Kearton, 6, 26 (top right); Shutterstock: Andy119, 14, 27 (top left), djv-photo, 12, 26 (bottom), Irene Elley, 10, 26 (middle right), Jasminschm, cover (eye), Linas Krisiukenas, 18, 27 (middle left), Patrick Jennings, 2-3, PeopleImages.com - Yuri A, 22, 27 (bottom left), Piotr Wawrzyniuk, cover, Pressmaster, 8, 26 (middle left), Richard Wozniak, 20, 27 (middle right), shaineast, design element (landscape), VanderWolf Images, 28, WDnet Creation, 4, 26 (top left)

Printed in the United States   6026

Who Am I?

There are 570 million farms around the world. Farmers raise animals and grow crops. Without farms, people wouldn't eat. I live on a farm. People like to visit farms too.

But what animal am I? Read the clues to find out.

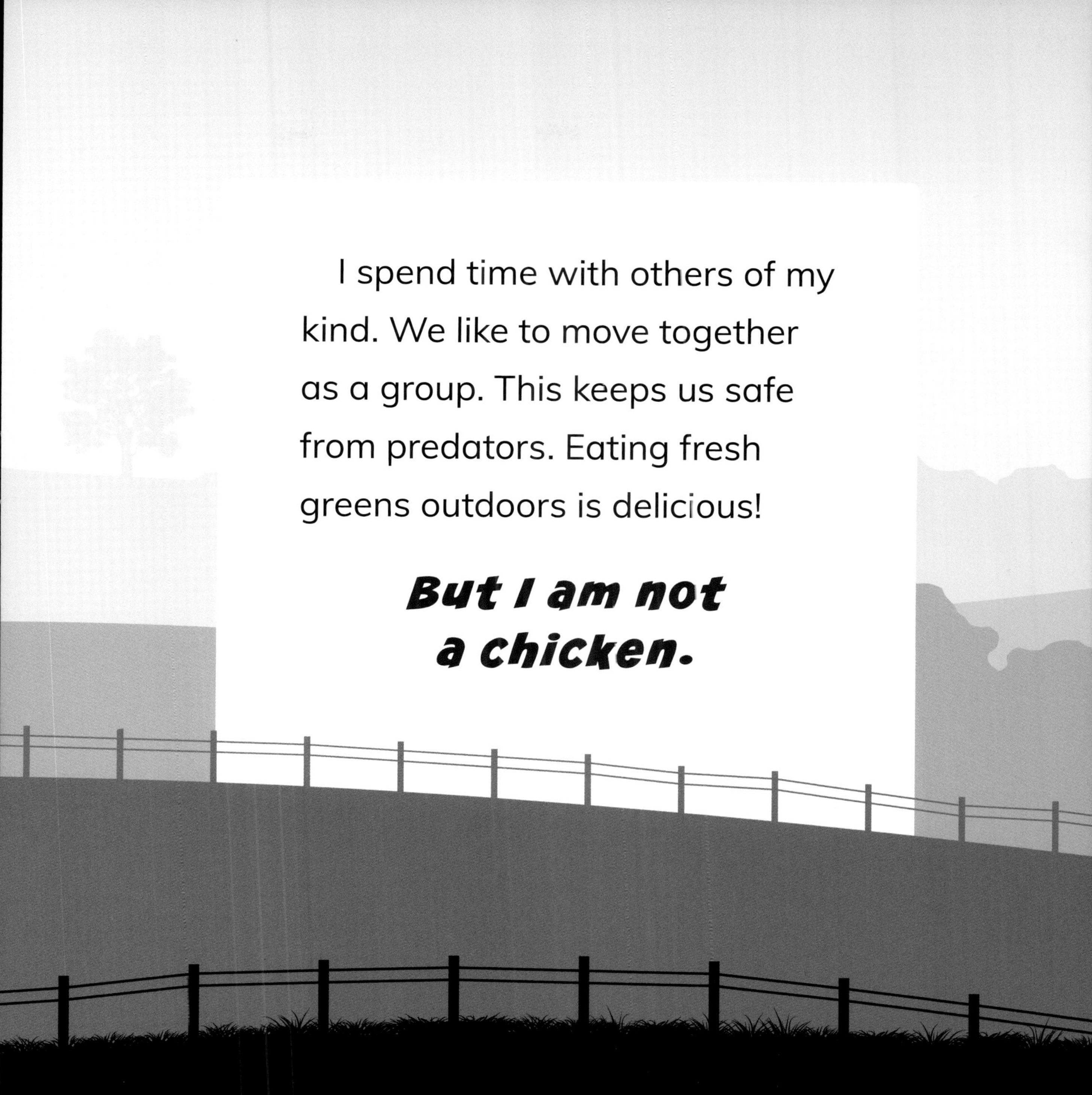

I spend time with others of my kind. We like to move together as a group. This keeps us safe from predators. Eating fresh greens outdoors is delicious!

But I am not a chicken.

Many people think we all look the same. You might have a hard time figuring who's who. But I can tell one friend from another by the noises they make.

But I am not a sheep.

My huge eyes can help me see more than 300 degrees around me. This means I can see behind or above without turning my head.

But I am not a rabbit.

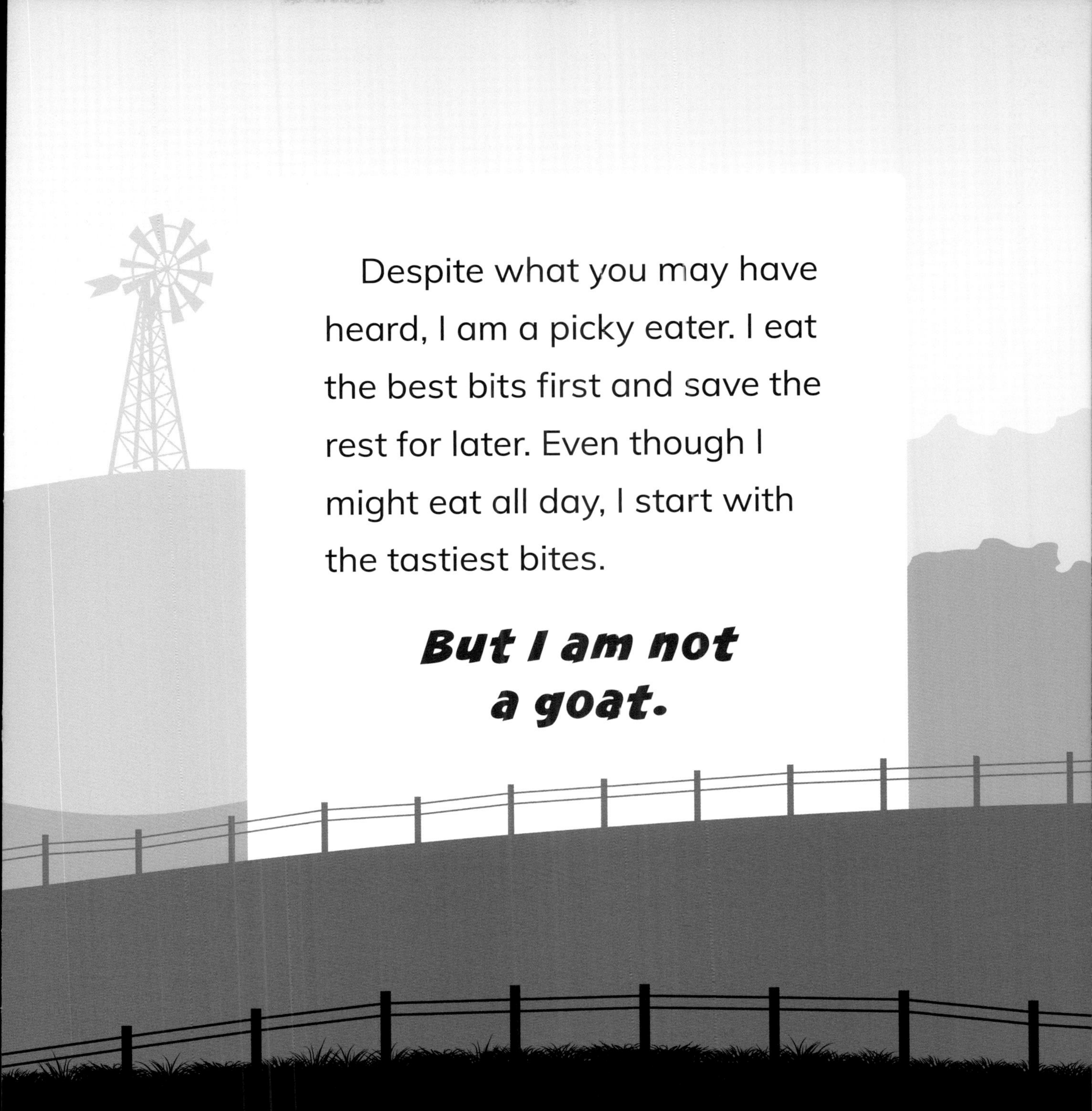

Despite what you may have heard, I am a picky eater. I eat the best bits first and save the rest for later. Even though I might eat all day, I start with the tastiest bites.

But I am not a goat.

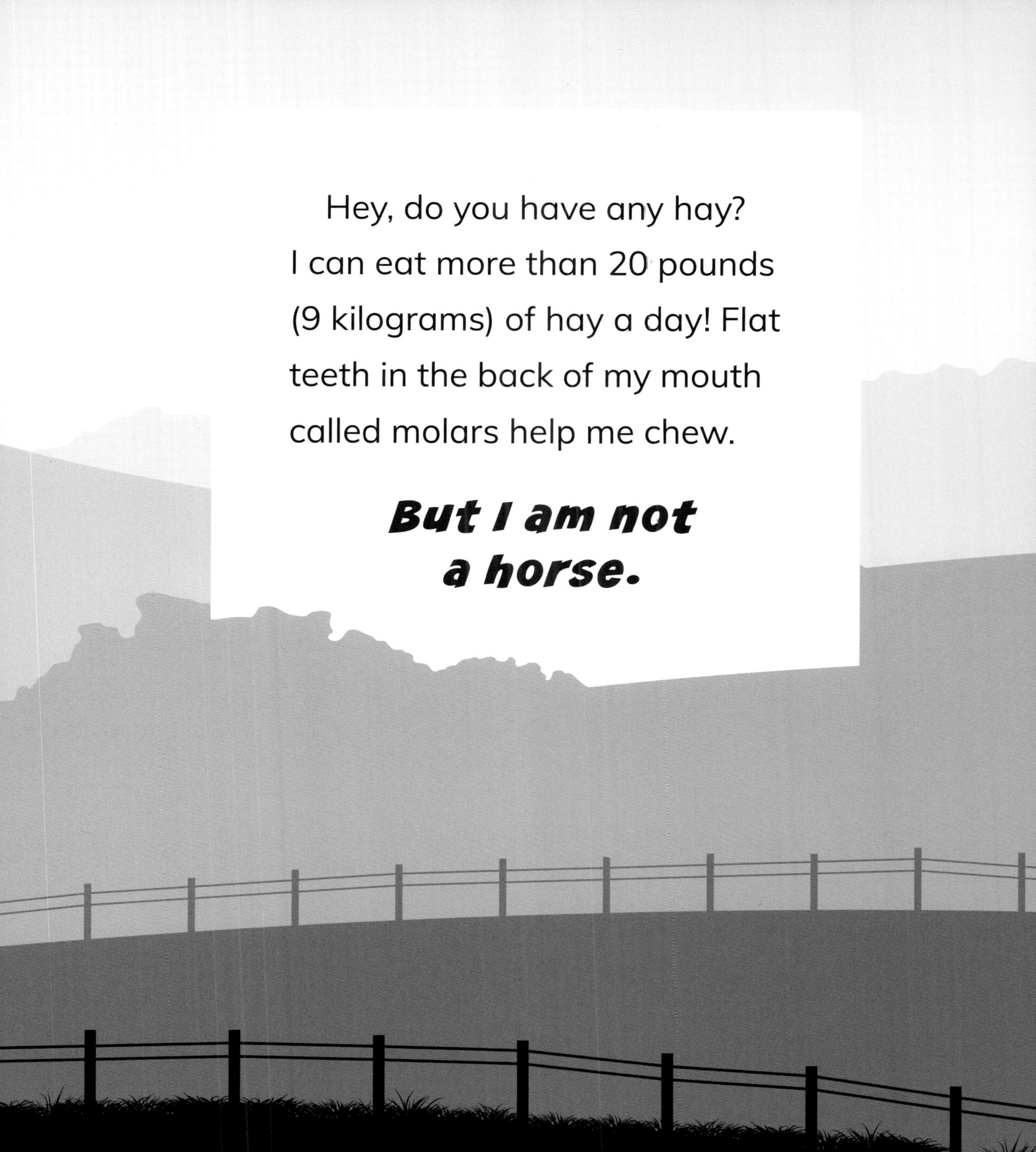

Hey, do you have any hay? I can eat more than 20 pounds (9 kilograms) of hay a day! Flat teeth in the back of my mouth called molars help me chew.

But I am not a horse.

Let's go for a swim! Getting from one side of the pond to the other is easy. My body is buoyant. That means it helps me float across the water.

But I am not a duck.

People love me. I'm very popular! Millions of my closest friends and family have homes around the world.

But I am not a cat.

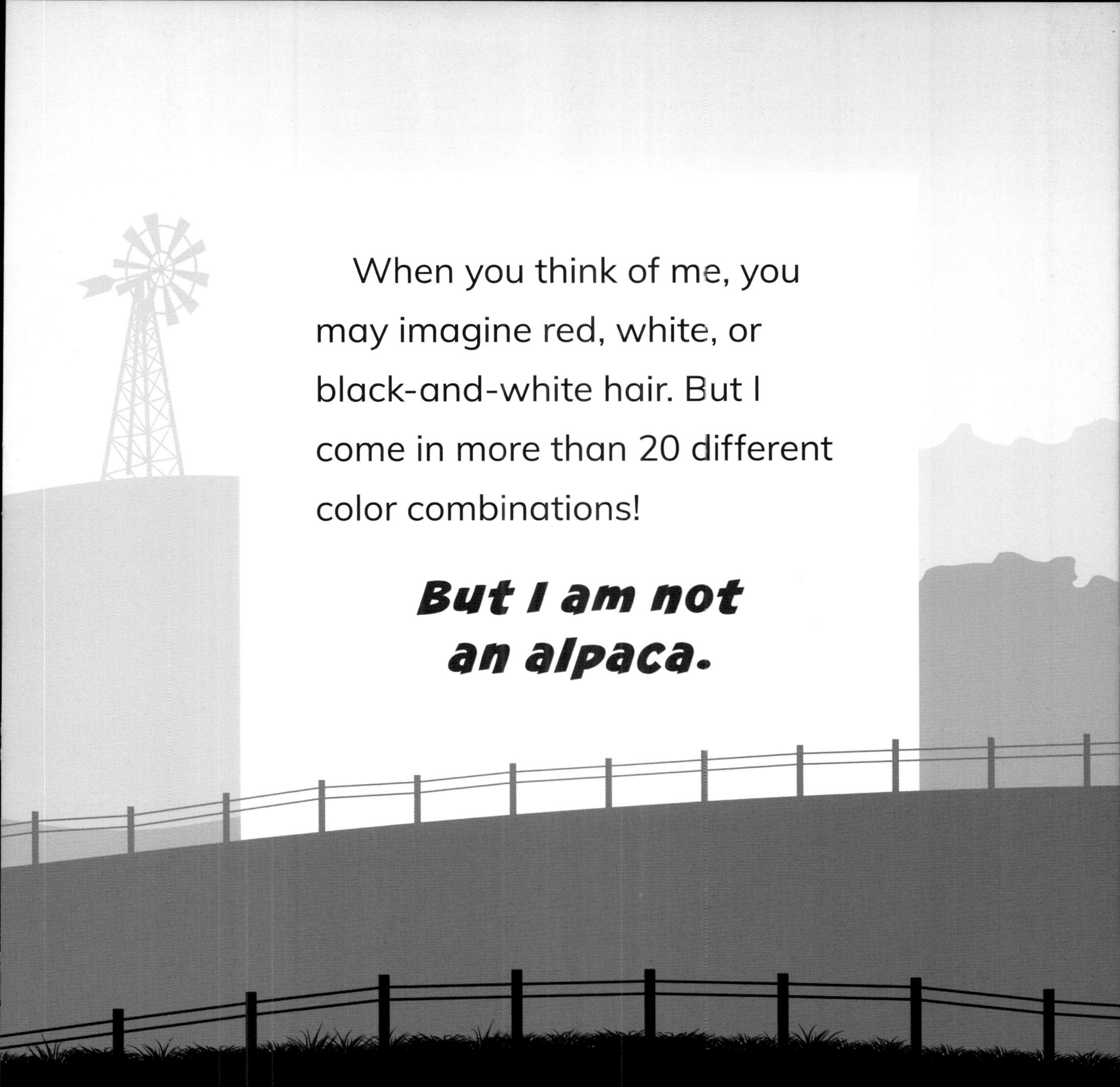
When you think of me, you may imagine red, white, or black-and-white hair. But I come in more than 20 different color combinations!

But I am not
an alpaca.

When you eat a lot, you poop a lot. People like to use my manure as fertilizer for their gardens. My poop helps your vegetables grow!

But I am not a turkey.

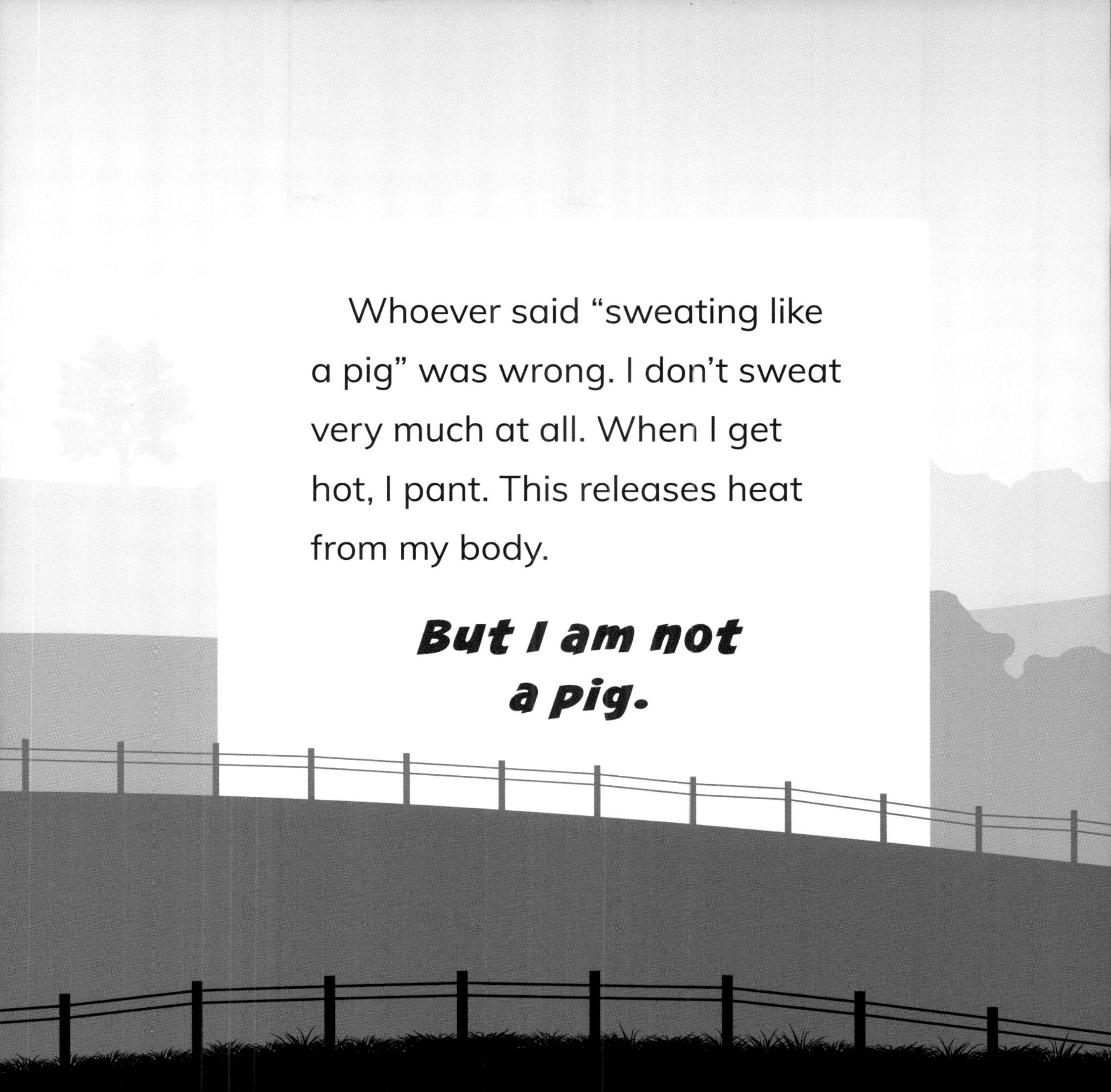

Whoever said "sweating like a pig" was wrong. I don't sweat very much at all. When I get hot, I pant. This releases heat from my body.

But I am not a pig.

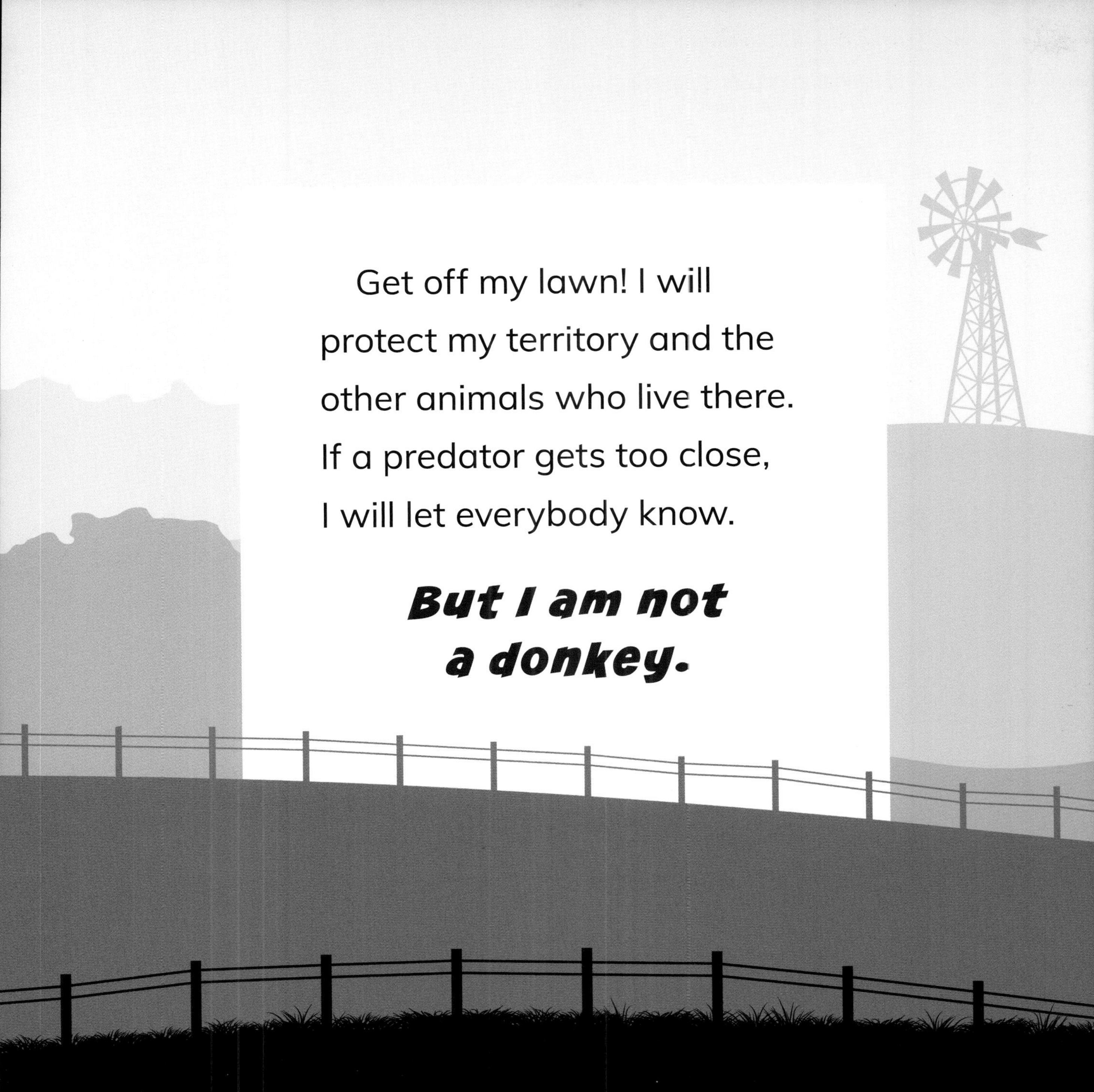

Get off my lawn! I will protect my territory and the other animals who live there. If a predator gets too close, I will let everybody know.

But I am not a donkey.

I am not a chicken

or a sheep

or a rabbit

or a goat

or a horse

or a duck

or a cat

or an alpaca

or a turkey

or a pig

or a donkey.

So what animal am I?

I am a cow!

I can be found around the world.
Where there are people, there are
probably cows. Cows are used
for milk, fur, meat, and manure.
It can be hard to tell one cow from
another. Cows eat all day long.

COOL FACTS ABOUT
COWS

Cows have 12-inch (30.5-centimeter)-long tongues. They use their long tongues to clean their noses.

Most of the milk in the world comes from cows. One cow can make 6 to 7 gallons (22.7 to 26.5 liters) of milk every day.

All cows are female. Males are bulls or steers. Before a cow has her first calf, she is called a heifer.

All cows can swim. They have strong legs and bodies that float easily.

Cow stomachs have four sections. Each section plays its own role. They chew and re-chew food to make sure it is fully digested.

Cows don't have top front teeth, so they can't bite and grab food. Instead, they use their tongues to tear grass. Then, they chew and swallow

Books in This Series

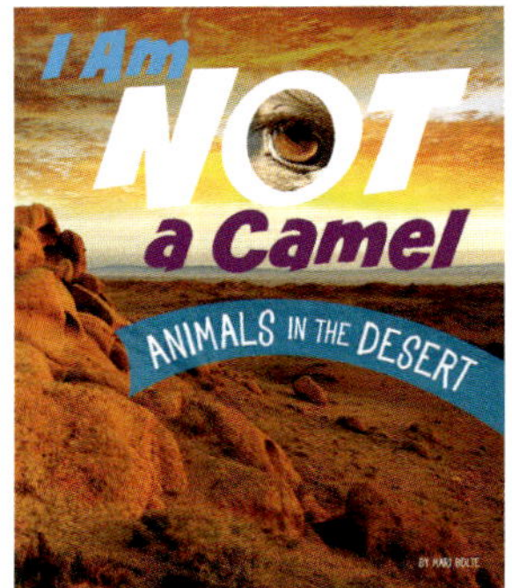

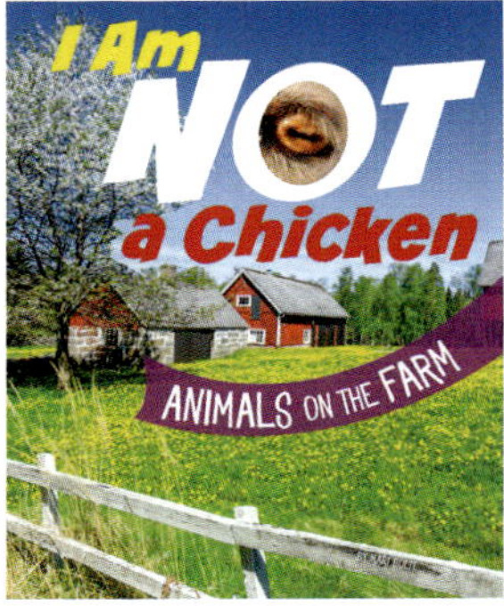

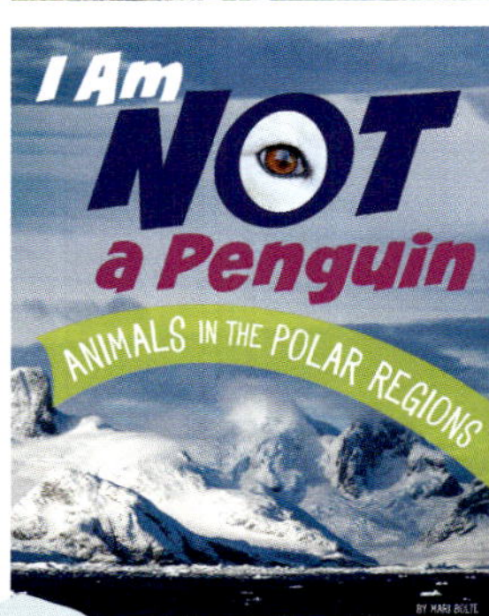

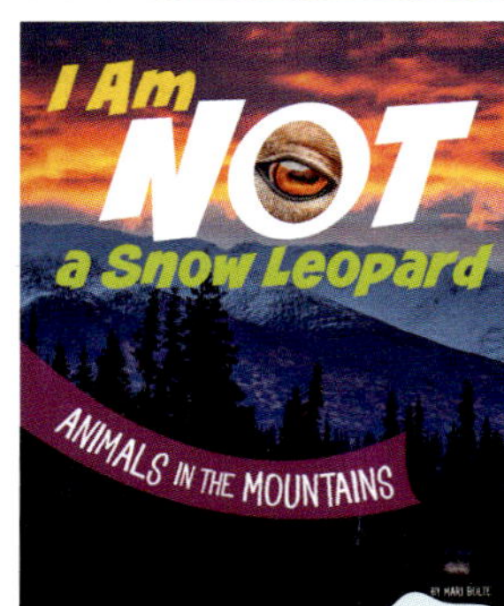

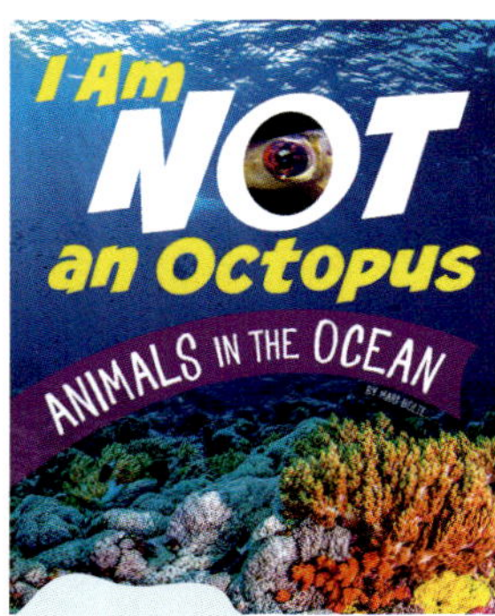

Author Bio

Mari Bolte is an author and editor of children's books on all sorts of subjects, from graphic novels about science to art projects to hands-on history. She lives in southern Minnesota in the middle of a forest full of animals.